HEROISM

HEROISM
an everyday person's guide to
ANYTHING-BUT-NORMAL LIVING

ERIC LUDY

Ellerslie
PRESS
WINDSOR, COLORADO

HEROISM: THE EVERYDAY PERSON'S GUIDE TO
ANYTHING-BUT-NORMAL LIVING
© 2015 by Eric Ludy

Published by Ellerslie Press
Windsor, Colorado
Ellerslie.com

Unless otherwise indicated, Scripture quotations are from:
The Holy Bible, New King James Version (nkjv) © 1984
by Thomas Nelson, Inc.

ISBN-10: 194359211X
ISBN-13: 9781943592111

Printed in the United States of America.

EricLudy.com

For Mikey.
You live out the contents of this book, and
you have brought Job 29 to life for your generation.
Oh, that God would raise up more men like you!

• • • • •

This book is dedicated to suffering children everywhere.

CONTENTS

Chapter One: Epic Living   9

Bravehearted Thots: Fizzle or Sizzle?   19

Chapter Two: A Hack in the House   21

Bravehearted Thots: About the Father's Business   33

Chapter Three: That's My Hudson   35

Bravehearted Thots: Sarandon versus Studd   48

Chapter Four: Starting with One   51

Bravehearted Thots: Kissing Babies for the Cameras   64

Chapter Five: Spiritual Employment   67

Let us not glide through this world and then slip quietly into heaven without having blown the trumpet loud and long for our Redeemer, Jesus Christ. Let us see to it that the devil will hold a thanksgiving service in hell when he gets the news of our departure from the field of battle.

C.T. Studd

England will do well when it transfers its affections from poodles and terriers to poor and destitute children.

Catherine Booth

CHAPTER ONE

EPIC LIVING

When I was eight, I invented a solar-powered car. America was facing an energy crisis in the late 1970s, and I for one was not going to sit idly by and let us go down the proverbial tubes.

The day my marvelous invention materialized was a hot one. It was one of those summer days that calls little boys to explore the wild outdoors, to search for buried treasure, or perhaps discover a slimy crawdad to satisfy their scientific curiosity. Yet though my eight-year-old lungs longed to suck in the fresh August air, an entire country's economic infrastructure hung woefully in the balance, and I felt a prick within my soul to do my part.

I purloined a sharpened pencil from my mother's collection and dug up a pile of drawing paper from the roll-top desk in the den, and I determinedly went to work. I must have worn that pencil down to a stub by the end of the day. My hair was tousled and my lips dried and caked from licking my lips in intense concentration for several straight hours.

I emerged from my makeshift office at around four in

the afternoon with one of those dazed da Vinci smirks upon my face, for I had done it: I had saved the world.

President Jimmy Carter didn't have to personally commission me to do this. He didn't have to offer me money, fame, or a position of power. I gave up an entire day of my summer vacation because I truly cared, and my imagination was fired up and ready to solve our nation's energy crisis.

I gave my all. I gave my best. I spent myself for my country.

Why?

Because that day I had something bigger than little Eric Ludy to live for, something grander than my own selfish pleasure to pursue. Creek beds, gold, crawdads, little green army men, climbing trees, flying kites, the continuing adventures of "Eric the Cowboy" — these could all wait, for there was something more important that needed my best energies and my best resources until all was made right with the world once more.

Unfortunately, my solar-powered car was nothing more than a little kid's piece of art. At the age of eight, I didn't understand that a mere drawing of a solar-powered car wouldn't actually solve the energy crisis. Blessed be those days of blissful ignorance and innocence! Yet thanks to my always-encouraging parents, I really did think I had saved the world that hot summer day back in 1979.

On that balmy day, little Eric Ludy had gone from being part of the problem to being part of the solution. He was not cowering in fear at the looming economic issues facing America; he was staring them in the face and offering his time, his resources, and his artistic talents for the betterment of mankind. As a result, he felt a surge of that strange and inexplicable happiness that courses through the veins of everyone who has ever done the same.

This book is built on a very simple premise: we all need to live for something bigger than ourselves. We need to be part of a story larger than us, a drama grander than our personal aches and pains. We need a blueprint for our existence that is greater than the one we ourselves can draw up. In short, we need to seek God's agenda for how our lives are supposed to be lived and what we are supposed to spend our time and energy pursuing.

In America, we suffer from a malady I call "puny living." Most of us spend twenty-three and three-quarters hours each and every day tending to our own life stories. And let's face it — our stories are not very grand. We spend our best energies, our best time, our best resources, and our best ideas on our smallish lives, hoping to somehow increase our net worth, upgrade our wheels, downgrade our stress, outpace our neighbors, and upstage our graduating class. The long and short of it is this: we are completely wasting this precious gift called life.

When I was eight, I tasted the pure and utter bliss of hero's work. To experience this taste, I didn't have to endure cruel torture and privation, storm a burning building, or rescue a drowning child. I merely had to give up my personal agenda in exchange for a much bigger one.

Not long ago, my wife, Leslie, and I were visiting Southern California. While there, we stepped out of a grocery store and ran smack into two young women with a cause. Their eyes were wide with enthusiasm, and their voices were strong with passion.

Their cause? Fifty whales off the shores of Japan.

11

These well-meaning women were spending their entire Saturday preaching to anyone willing to listen about the atrocities being committed against these poor humpback whales and how something must be done.

Now don't get me wrong. I have only positive feelings about these magnificent, charismatic creatures. Whales are amazing!

However, let's consider the fact that there are 163 million children around the world that are orphaned and in desperate need of help at this very moment. Fifty whales just don't seem important in comparison.

There are more human slaves today than there were one hundred years ago when William Wilberforce fought his noble battle with Parliament to end this brutal injustice. There are scores of little girls between the ages of six and eleven being sold into slavery as prostitutes in countries all around the world. There are little boys being forced to kill their parents and siblings and become soldiers in the Ugandan "liberation" armies. There are more than four thousand little children who are homeless, parentless, and living in a single dump in Guatemala. There are tens of thousands of kids in Brazil hiding from death squads seeking to kill the "orphan vermin."

Maybe if there were fifty million capable foot-soldiers actively fighting for the cause of the oppressed, enslaved, and orphaned around the world, I could see the importance of turning our attentions toward the suffering of fifty humpback whales off the coast of Japan. But that is simply not the case.

I'm not trying to knock someone for fighting on behalf of the whales. In a fashion, it's noble and it's right. But it is akin to trying to rescue the captain's personal trunk when the entire ship is sinking.

We need to open our eyes to the true scope of the situation we find ourselves in here on earth. We are suffering from puny living, and it's affected our eyesight. We aren't seeing the real issues because we can't see outside of our own little universes.

Heroes Wanted

I'm a Christian and I make no bones about it. I am all about following Jesus Christ and His agenda. His agenda is huge, it's grand, and it's a steak dinner for the imagination. There is nothing puny about God's intention for His children. Yet perhaps the greatest perpetrators of puny living in the past one hundred years have been Christian folk. It's sad to say, but Christianity is deserving of most of the criticism it receives these days. The church has tried to fit into the world and make itself appealing rather than turning the world upside down and transforming it. Christianity in its truest most historic sense is all about "epic living."

For one entire day when I was eight, I tasted epic living. I was caught up in the cause of saving the world. What I tasted that day is what every believer was meant to taste every single day for a lifetime. Imagine waking up each day feeling a divine urgency to give your best energies, your best time, your best resources, and your best ideas to something other than yourself. That's Christianity in its most elemental form. That's the secret to a life of ever-increasing satisfaction.

The problems facing humanity are much bigger than oil embargos, whaling, illegal immigration, and global warming. Thirty thousand children are dying this very day due to something as basic as the lack of clean water. And yet our best and brightest are spending themselves on puny convictions and puny causes.

A truly Christian life is one that demonstrates to the world what Jesus would look like, talk like, and live like if He were walking the earth today (Ephesians 5:1–2). A Christian life is nothing more than an everyday human existence given over to the operation and control of the very Spirit of God (Romans 8:6). In other words, it's God who is living, not me (Galatians 2:20). It's God who is talking, not me. It's God who is deciding where to go and how to get there, not me.

Jesus Christ is interested in your life — *All of it.* He wants every moment of your existence, from now to the end of eternity, to be spent as He deems fit. He wants to turn your paltry little life into something extraordinary. But to do that, He has to own the entirety of it, with no strings attached. He won't suffer any *ifs*, *ands*, or *buts*. He will rescue you, He will cleanse you, and He will make your life work — but only if you are willing to give up all control to Him.

What would God be doing if you truly gave Him control over your life?

If you are not a Christian, I ask you to please forgive those of us who are not providing an answer to that question with our lives. We've muddled the answer to that question to the point where there are now seventy-six different answers from seventy-six different pulpits every Sunday morning. What has happened to the church? How did we arrive at the place where Christianity is about *us* — our lives, our retirement plans, our futures, our reputations, our personal comfort — without even a mumbled protest from the pews?

Christianity isn't only about what you know and who you know — it's also about how you respond in obedience to whom you know. If you are not directing your energies toward that which is the heart of Jesus — the rescuing of human souls and the deliverance of human lives — then, like nuclear waste, you will end up actually corroding the world about you. Jesus said it this way: "He that is not with me is against me," and, "The Son of man is come to seek and to save that which was lost" (Luke 11:23, 19:10).

Our God is all about action. He's all about doing the thing that needs to be done. He's all about giving. (Doesn't it say something about that in John 3:16?)

God is in the business of delivering justice and mercy, setting captives free, bringing health to the sick, clearing the debts of the poor, and breaking the shackles of slavery. God burns with fury when He sees the weak and the little ones being exploited. He cries with indignation when He sees child prostitution in Thailand, abortion in America, death squads murdering street children in Brazil, and little boys and girls struggling to live in a garbage dump in Central America.

Our God is not passive, and He is certainly not unfeeling. He has entrusted His foot-soldiers here on earth with the job of expressing His indignation, His compassion, His generosity, and His love here in this physical world. Christians are supposed to be His hands, His feet, His voice, and His response to these atrocities in the natural realm.

If it appears God is doing nothing to halt these horrors,

the blame for inactivity falls squarely on the shoulders of those of us entrusted to be His representatives. It's Christians that bear the onus of culpability. We are the ones commissioned to carry out God's epic agenda, and if we fritter our lives away pursuing puny goals and do nothing to stop these horrors, then we will stand before God in the end with a stain of responsibility upon our souls.

God's agenda is to seek and save that which is lost, that which is broken, and that which is oppressed and enslaved. But if God's children won't carry out His agenda, who will?

The world is waiting for you and me to begin to live out and practice what we preach. Christianity will be nothing more than a byword as long as those of us that call ourselves by such a regal name sit by and live puny lives while the world about us is ravaged by evil. But when Christians once again take up the epic agenda of God, the world will sit up and take notice. For wherever there were Christians who boldly carried the torch of poured-out love, justice, and compassion, the church multiplied and was added to daily. May Christianity once again be the world-altering force it was in those days when Christ first deposited His very life and fire into the souls of His followers.

This book is designed for all of us, including myself, who have suffered from the malady of puny living. So if you are interested in doing something more with your energies and resources than filling out forms and writing checks ... if you are ready to be part of something much grander than yourself ... if you are tired of a crusty version of faith that merely sits in pews, listening to sermons and passing the offering plates, then keep reading. You are about to discover the magnificence and marvel of a bigger, more thrilling, more rewarding vision of life.

May the glory and power of Christ be seen in and through you and me. May the lost hear the hope of the Bravehearted Gospel through our mouths. May the hungry be fed with our hands. May the orphans be rescued by our valor. May we break the shackles of the oppressors with our passion for justice.

Is it not a serious thought that many clean-living, decent persons, against whom no overt act of wrongdoing can be charged, may yet be deeply guilty and inwardly stained with the sin that does not show, the sin of silence and inaction? There are moral situations where it is immoral to say nothing and basely immoral to do nothing.

A.W. Tozer

I have fought the good fight, I have finished the race, I have kept the faith.

2 Timothy 4:7

BRAVEHEARTED THOTS

FIZZLE OR SIZZLE?

You are, in a sense, immortal.

I realize that sounds a bit like something out of a Tolkien novel. But seventy-five trillion years from now, after the empires of this earth have faded from existence, you will still be around. And yet, the seventy-five years you have *right now* will shape your eternal destiny.

Seventy-five years define the next seventy-five trillion.

Just imagine that a million years from now an angel asks you what you did with your life, how you advanced the kingdom of heaven, how you championed the cause of God. What will your answer be? Will you and I be able to say that we were about our Father's business, that we ran a good race and fought a good fight?

It's time to get down to business.

No one can lead farther than he himself has gone.

A.W. Tozer

Charity — giving to the poor — is an essential part of Christian morality. . . . I do not believe one can settle how much we ought to give. I am afraid the only safe rule is to give more than is comfortable. In other words, if our expenditures on comforts, luxuries, amusements, etc. is up to the standard common among those with the same income as our own, we are probably giving too little.

C.S. Lewis
Mere Christianity

CHAPTER TWO

A HACK IN THE HOUSE

My Granddad Ludy was famous for being a straight-shooter. His values included sound doctrine, the economics of Ronald Reagan, Apple Jacks cereal, and fine music — not necessarily in that order.

I was nineteen and an aspiring musician. I couldn't read a chord chart or pick up a harmony line if my life hung in the balance, but I possessed a kind of artsy attitude that I thought might cover up my musical ignorance. An artsy attitude can go a long way with many people today, but my granddad was a stickler for authenticity and quality. And whereas I fooled some into thinking I could be the next Sinatra, my granddad was not hoodwinked.

When I was growing up, family reunions were always a place where the up-and-coming generation could show off their talents to earn easy compliments and praise. You could stink and still receive a warm round of applause and exclamations of awe and wonder. Granddad Ludy would usually sit by quietly and hold his tongue. In hindsight I'm almost positive that my grandmother threatened to make him sleep on the couch if he opened his mouth and muttered a word of criticism.

Looking back, I'm kind of proud of my granddad. He witnessed some rather paltry stuff and did a pretty good job sitting there and acting like he missed it. However, as hard as it might have been for him to hold his tongue when it came to skits of regurgitated Jell-O, horribly off-pitch serenades, and dismal performances by the less-than-impressive thespians in our family tree, he just couldn't hold it in any longer when it came to his grandson Eric.

Granddad had high hopes for me. He spent hour upon hour trying to woo my musical taste buds away from Jon Bon Jovi, Billy Joel, and Peter Cetera and redirect them toward Antonio Vivaldi, Maurice Ravel, and Pyotr Tchaikovsky. He would sit at the old piano in his study and play a Stravinski masterpiece as if he were basking in the aromas of a Parisian bakery, and then look back at me and say, "Do you hear it?" He wanted so desperately for me to share in his passion for great music. He wanted me to hear what he was hearing. Unfortunately, I never heard anything. I couldn't get past the musty smell of his little study and the yellowed pages of music from which he played. The antique "noise" held no meaning for a young man trying to reach the modern culture.

Well, it was the 1990 edition of the family reunion talent show, and I was, like any truly humble musician, trying to act as if I didn't want to perform for the family. At the age of nineteen, I was a bit too grown up for the talent show — at least, that was my line. But when the begging began in earnest, I slowly rose from my chair and shuffled awkwardly to the piano, shaking my head as if I couldn't believe they had talked me into this.

I sat down and placed my fingers upon the keys. And I played. I played with passion! I played with gusto! I played the one song in my repertoire I knew would leave them wanting more. And there sat my Granddad Ludy grimacing and squirming in his seat. I can just see my grandmother squeezing his hand and whispering, "Honey, don't you dare!" But this was his *grandson* disgracing the Ludy name and the very concept of music itself. Something had to be done. And if my granddad had to sleep a night on the couch, so be it!

I remember receiving some hearty encouragement later that evening after my two-song set. I shook hands with a gracious fan and said, "Thanks so much! I really appreciate it, Uncle Harold!" And there in the shadows stood Granddad Ludy. His countenance was serious, his eyebrows knitted in consternation. He was probably thinking to himself, *I'll bring that one oversized patchwork quilt to the couch with me tonight, and I probably won't sleep half bad.*

"Hey, Granddad!" I said, completely ignorant of what was about to transpire.

Without a greeting, he cleared his throat and said, "Eric, you play the piano like a hack!"

Honestly, I don't remember my response. I was so taken aback, so bewildered. I mean, who in the world other than Simon Cowell really has the guts to tell a musician to his face what they really think? And this was my granddad! And my granddad knew music. He knew how that piano was supposed to sound. He had spent more than eighty years studying, playing, and listening to the instrument, and if anyone could tell a wanna-be "hack" from a genuine master of the keys (*gulp*), it would be my granddad.

"Eric, you play the piano like a hack!"

What do you do when confronted with the truth? Yes, I realize it will take you aback and bewilder you for the moment. But I'm talking about what you do after that moment has passed and you are standing face to face with the reality that the performance of your life was nothing more than a self-centered, second-rate charade.

"Eric, you play the piano like a hack!"

I turned those words over and over in my mind. At first I chafed at his audacity. I mean, who was he to say something like that to his grandson? What kind of granddad was he anyway? But as time passed, I allowed his words to sink in, and I began to objectively reevaluate my supposed musical abilities.

It took me a few years, but I finally admitted to myself that Granddad was right: I was a hack. I was a pretender, a showman, a wanna-be. This was not an easy realization to come to, especially since the musical novices around me all thought the seeming talent I possessed was actually impressive. The average person watching my act may not have known that I didn't really have a clue what I was doing on those piano keys, but a real professional would certainly have recognized that my unorthodox style and oversized personality were little more than a cover-up for something that was lacking.

There's No Shortcut to Excellence

Our world is loaded with hacks — individuals looking for a shortcut to excellence. Like me, hacks attempt to mimic greatness by pasting a few accouterments to their act in order to pull the wool over everyone's eyes. For example, I tried to play the piano like Bruce Hornsby by swaying emotively as my fingers plunked on the keys. I tried to sing like Steve Perry by singing uncomfortably high (the sound resembled a dying magpie). I even tried to squint my eyes in a manner reminiscent of Sean Connery, hoping all the girls would confuse me with James Bond. I wanted my name to somehow get mixed up in conversation with the names of accomplished performers, but I didn't want to have to actually do the work to become accomplished.

The sad thing is I carried this same hack mentality into my faith. I wanted a shortcut to spiritual excellence. I tried to mimic Christ's greatness by tacking on a few religious accouterments to my Christian act. *This Christ-imitation stuff can't be that difficult*, I remember thinking. So I attempted to speak in a humble-sounding voice. I worked Scripture references into my conversations to get people to think I spent a lot of time studying the Word. I took every opportunity to pray aloud in groups, hoping to convince people of my lofty spirituality.

Sound familiar? The truth is many of us in the church today are spiritual hacks.

I'm sorry to be so blunt. Believe me, I know how it feels. But this kind of hack mentality must be recognized for what it is. A hack takes something noble and sacred and beautiful, and marginalizes it, diminishing its power. A hack takes a gourmet meal and reduces it to a Cup o' Noodles and says, "It's all just food. What's the difference, really?" A hack takes fine china and diminishes it to paper plates and Styrofoam cups. A hack takes the artistic doodles of a third-grader and proclaims them to be as significant and valuable as a Rembrandt just because both were sketched in the Netherlands.

I'm not trying to say that the hacks among us are purposefully trying to lower the standards of the Christian life; it's just that many of us have never seen the real thing with which to compare our two-cent, mediocre version. Most hacks think their "self-centered, second-rate charade" of a Christian life is a great work of art. After all, isn't that what our friends and relatives have told us?

But the Bible speaks of joy that is full, exceeding, abundant, and not in the least bit conditional on our circumstances. Our joy is supposed to be like a Cheerio in milk — unsinkable. If that's true, then what is this "joy" that most modern Christians are lugging around? Could it be that it's nothing more than a four-year-old's rendition of "Chopsticks"?

There's a hack in the house.

The Bible proclaims that true Christians can be identified by a love that is wholly selfless. Supposedly, we are cheek-turners when struck, extra-mile-walkers when asked, cloak-givers when requested, and foot-washers in everyday situations. We are ready to forgive, without grievance and without being asked. Whether stabbed with unkind words or with daggers, we bleed grace, patience, gentleness, mercy, and kindness. And this is the way we are to live *all* the time — not just once a week.

There's a hack in the house.

God calls us to live lives of total and complete faith, without an ounce of fear, fretting, or anxiety. We are supposed to have a resolute confidence in our God's ability to provide and never budge from this stance even when by all natural appearances it would seem that our God has forgotten us. We are to be unshakable, indefatigable, and immovable in our trust.

There's a hack in the house.

However, just because many of us are hacks doesn't mean we aren't real Christians. But we aren't living the lives our Master intended. We are still making a form of music, and to the untrained ear — those who aren't familiar with the Bible and the triumphant faith we are called to — our music might even sound somewhat impressive. But the fact that we can mimic the angels with our swaying and singing cannot hide the fact that we are little more than pretenders.

The Heroic Alternative

My granddad was a master musician, and his standard of excellence exposed me as a musical fraud. The master reveals the hack, for a true master of any craft cannot and will not allow his discipline to be eroded by fraudulent artisans. The master is compelled to preserve and pass along the standard of perfection from generation to generation. And if there is some kid out there parading about as if he has redefined the craft, then the master is willing to sleep on the couch for the night to make it clear there's a hack in the house. All of us need a master in our lives in order to show us the way toward perfection.

Jesus was a Hero, not a hack. He was the genuine article: the perfect reflection of the Master (John 14:9). He was, and always will be, the one true template for the heroic life each and every one of us ought to be living (1 Peter 2:21).

As believers, we are meant to be world-changers—men and women who turn society on its head. And yet most of us are having a difficult time shifting our lives into first gear, let alone becoming instruments of hope and rescue for the dying world around us.

Andrea Amati is the father of the fine Cremonese violin, the ultimate music machine. Amati was a master. He knew what a violin was supposed to look like, sound like, and feel like. Why? Because he created them. He gave the modern violin its distinctive profile.

If you want to become a master maker of violins, then you seek out a master violin maker like Amati and become his apprentice. However, if you want to become a master at changing the world, then you must seek out the Master World-Changer Himself.

Jesus brought demons to their knees.

His birth came to define the historic human calendar.

He defeated death itself.

He unshackled humanity from enslavement to sin.

He is the ultimate Hero, who gave up His life in order to secure ours.

You want to change the world? Become an apprentice of Jesus Christ. Live how He lived, love like He loved, serve like He served (Philippians 2:5–7). Do exactly as He did.

What was Jesus doing? He was about His Father's business. He didn't live for the applause of men, nor did He live in fear of them. He lived to do the will of the One who sent Him (John 6:38).

This book is short, and it's short for a reason. It's been written to say something quick and say it strong.

We must become like the Master.

But there's a hack in the house. And no matter how hard we try to mimic His brilliance and brawn, His holiness and humility, His purity and perfection, we simply cannot do it. No matter how hard we try, we are hacks. Frauds. Posers. He's amazing. And (*gulp*) we are not.

However, this is a book about heroism. It's about planting the heroism of Jesus Christ squarely in the hearts, lives, attitudes, and behaviors of the redeemed. In other words, the fact that we are hacks, frauds, and posers is not the final statement on the matter.

What's needed in today's church isn't a new Gospel but a complete one. Jesus didn't merely accomplish the salvation of His saints from an eternity in hell. He didn't just purchase us forgiveness on that tree. He did something even better: He purchased us (1 Corinthians 6:19–20).

He turned our house upside down, cleaned us up, and purged us of all that would hinder Him from moving in and calling our bodies His earthly home.

The Gospel just isn't the Gospel until the notion of *God inside us* is proclaimed.

You see, you (the hack) can't live the Master's life. You can't imitate it or muster up the resolve to follow it. He's holy and you aren't. He's perfect and you aren't. He's supernatural and you are bound by everything natural.

However, when you grab hold of the purpose of the Cross, you suddenly realize that Jesus Christ wants more than your appreciation—He wants your very life. He wants to move in, overtake you, and seize control for His glory (Romans 8:9).

Why? So that you can be about the Father's business. Jesus said, "As the Father has sent Me, I also send you" (John 20:21).

Jesus was a Hero. And the Father's business is a labor of love, otherwise known as Hero's Work.

It's preaching the Gospel, setting captives free, delivering the poor, clothing the naked, bringing the orphaned into families, making the widow's heart sing for joy, healing the sick, comforting the weak, and breaking the grip of evildoers and rescuing their victims.

But to fulfill this labor of love, to accomplish this Hero's work, you must allow yourself to be overtaken by the Great Hero. You must become His body. Your eyes must become His eyes. Your mouth, His mouth. Your ears, His ears. Your mind, His mind. Your hands, His hands. Your heart, His heart. Your feet, His feet.

You must begin to look at what He is looking at, talk about what He's talking about, listen to what He's listening to, and think about precisely what He is thinking about. You must wash the feet of those He's seeking to serve, feel the very burdens and aches that His heart is feeling, and go to the most destitute and darkened places where He is desiring to shine His light.

This is Christianity. It's a holy God making a holy people by invading them with His Holy Spirit and causing a holy reformation of individuals, marriages, families, churches, businesses, and society, in that order.

Heroes are not made through grit, self-determination, or by pulling themselves up by the proverbial bootstraps. True Heroes are the product of Jesus Christ's grace, His divine and loving determination, and His pulling us up from the depths of our sin.

So for all us hacks in the house, there is hope. The Master of Worlds is ready to enter in, seize our houses, and make something of our lives.

Remember, my giving will be rewarded not by how much
I have but by how much I had left.

A.W. Tozer

"Did you not know that I must be about My
Father's business?"

Luke 2:49

"I have glorified You on the earth. I have finished the work
which You have given Me to do."

John 17:4

ABOUT THE FATHER'S BUSINESS

The Father's business is currently short on staff.

So here's my best rendition of career counseling: if you haven't done it yet, set up a meeting with God. Sit down with Him and have a serious talk about your life. Your side of the conversation ought to sound something like this:

"So, God, I hear You have a business and that You're looking for laborers here on earth. I understand that my life is not my own and that I've been bought with a price and that I am Yours. In light of this, I want my remaining years on earth to be all about Your business. I want to do everything that You intended my singular life to accomplish. Like Christ, I want to be able to say when I breathe my last breath, 'It is finished!'"

You may be untrained, unqualified, and unkempt. But if you come to God and express such a desire, you will have yourself a job. And you will find yourself working for the greatest employer in the universe.

I am a missionary, heart and soul. God had an only Son, and He was a missionary and a physician. A poor, poor imitation of Him I am, or wish to be. In this service I hope to live; in it I wish to die.

David Livingstone

CHAPTER THREE

THAT'S MY HUDSON

I'm a father.

Let me say it again, but this time I want you to imagine a gigantic grin on my face and a pool of sentimental tears in my dark-brown eyes.

I'm a father.

There is nothing quite like being a father.

Nothing causes emotion to well in my throat and a smile to crease my face like meditating on my precious children.

Leslie and I were married ten years before children arrived on the scene. Then God, with a wink and smile, piled four little chunker-doodles on top of our life in the subsequent four years. By June 2009, we had four kiddos aged four and under. It was almost like God was saying, "You've got some catching up to do, Ludy!"

I can't say that it's been all that easy. Kids are cute with their button noses, diapered bottoms, and tiny voices, but their behavior isn't always cute. The Bible promises that "foolishness is bound up in the heart of a child" (Proverbs 22:15), and I can personally attest that it's not a pretty picture when this foolishness rears its ugly head. But despite the challenges, there is nothing quite like being a father.

My kids linger playfully in my heart when I'm trying to act put-together and professional, crawling through my thoughts in the middle of important business meetings. When I'm preparing a sermon, I want to talk about them. When I'm writing a blog, I want to mention something cute they did that day. And when I'm trying to come up with a good teaching illustration, I can think of no better proverb than one involving my precious little ones.

I cry more now that I have kids. Some are tears of pain or heartache, but most are tears of pure affection and delight. They're tears that say, "Can we somehow push the pause button, God, so that I can fully cherish these glorious, short-lived days of their youth?"

It's natural for me, as a father, to love my kids and take delight in them. It's normal for me to concern myself with their well-being. If they are hurting, I hurt. If they are struggling, I'm struggling. And if they are happy, I'm happy.

Then in November 2007, God showed me something about fatherhood that forever changed me.

Wake Up!

Though I dearly love my children and would suffer greatly on their behalf, until recently there was a limit to my love. This strange limitation hindered my affection, care, and love from reaching beyond the walls of my own home. I would not hesitate to shed tears over the pain of my own children, but I had only dry eyes for the plight of any children who were not my own. It's not that I didn't care about their circumstances; it's that I was unable to *feel*. I was grieved to hear about children who suffered from hunger or oppression, but I was not moved to the point of action. I wasn't upset to the point of getting involved. I wasn't distressed to the point of lying awake at night.

I was largely numb to the problem.

And up until that November, I thought this was completely normal. After all, they weren't *my* kids.

Imagine for a moment if the wealthiest man on earth gave you unlimited access to his bank account. Sounds great, doesn't it? But what if your understanding was that "unlimited" meant "no more than $100"? You would almost certainly claim the $100 and probably be very happy about the extra cash in your pocket. But how much more would you be missing out on?

As a father, I have found access to something very beautiful and dear in my relationship with my children. It's a depth of care and affection that bewilders me. I would gladly suffer pain to prevent them from experiencing that pain for themselves. I would claw through a concrete wall to rescue them if they were in danger. But that is only the first $100. God was showing me there was so much more.

I remember the day my life turned upside down. I was on the phone, interviewing a missionary from Liberia. Her words were poignant and deeply convicting. She was describing the suffering in her country, and I was moved, startled, and deeply grieved. I remember her saying, "We just need Christians to come and give their lives, Eric. We have so many orphans and not enough hands and feet."

She told me about a little four-year-old boy sitting on the side of the road. She said, "There are children all around us, like him, that we just can't reach. We don't have the resources, the space, or the staff. So this boy sits there starving to death with no one to comfort him, feed him, clothe him, or house him. He's dying, Eric, and it would appear that no one on earth even cares."

I cringed as I listened. I really did feel bad for this boy. But to be honest, it was a distant sort of grief, not a personal grief. In other words, it was the sort of grief you might feel watching the evening news and hearing about a crisis in Japan's stock market or an investigation into human trafficking in Cambodia.

After the phone call, I shook my head in disbelief that such things were happening, and I prayed to God to somehow intervene on behalf of this little one. But afterward, I went back to business as usual. Somehow, even after hearing about a situation so desperate, I was able to return to my work and be focused and productive.

In the middle of the night, I was awakened.

I sat up straight in bed, and it seemed that a question hanging in the air pressed itself into my heart. My mind was filled with a picture of that little four-year-old boy sitting on the side of the road in Liberia. And the question that God had posed boomed into my soul: *Eric, what if that was Hudson?*

Hudson is my oldest child. At that time he, too, was four years old.

I was staggered by the question. Just the thought of

my son's enduring such depravation was more than my heart could handle. I didn't want to think such a thought. But the question continued to reverberate through my heart and soul.

What if that was Hudson?

Without hesitation I knew the answer.

If that abandoned little boy were Hudson, I would beat down every wall and slash through every obstacle to reach my son. There would be no delays, no second-guessing, no trifling over the petty cares of home and work. I would be on the first plane to Liberia. And if for some reason I was paralyzed or otherwise prevented from going myself, I would call up all my friends and beg them to go and do for my son that which his aching father desired to do for him.

I sat there in the dark, my face awash with shock, and I saw the Father's heart for that little four-year-old boy.

Eric, that is My Hudson!

I could hear Him challenging my soul to expand to the height, breadth, and depth of the heavenly call. It was as if He were saying, "Eric, I have a son over in Liberia. And I'm calling up all those who say they are my friends. I'll give you the coordinates, and I'll supply the airfare. I'll provide you with everything you need for the task — but I need you to get to him and be a father to him."

It was as if God were saying, "Remove the $100 limit on your fatherhood, Lucy! Draw from My unlimited depths of love and share in the burdens of My heart. Eric, I am looking for a man who is willing to feel what I am feeling — one who is willing to go and do that which I would go and do if I were there. For, Eric,

I am there through you. I am a Father to the fatherless in and through you. Remember, you are My body."

Our Tradition

Nearly every night prior to dozing off, Leslie and I remember each of our children. That might sound sort of strange, but let me explain.

The "remembering" goes something like this: I kick things off by saying, "Remember Avy Rosie?" Avonlea is our youngest, and at the time of this writing she was two years old.

This is Leslie's cue. But before she responds, the two of us will picture little Avy in our mind's eyes, with her crazy Shirley Temple head of curls and her spunky little attitude, and we will both laugh. Then Leslie will bring up something cute, hilarious, or otherwise fantastic that Avy did that day.

"I was cuddling with her in the chair tonight," Leslie recalls with a smile, "and Avy looked up at me and whispered, with a conspiratorial tone, 'Momma, I'm weally four.'"

We both chuckle at this and then spend a few moments cherishing how precious our little pumpkin truly is.

A few seconds later, I say, "Remember Dubby-Dooey?" Dubby-Dooey's formal name is Kipling, and he is seven months older than Avy, adopted at birth.

"When we were out at the play set today," recounts Leslie, "he saw a grasshopper and called it a 'hopper-grass.'"

Again, we cherish the hilarity of our little one and savor the sweetness of the thought.

"Remember Harper Grace?" I ask. Harper, four years old

at the time of this writing, was adopted from South Korea. Leslie laughs as she thinks about something Harper did that day. "Her tummy was growling before lunch, and she asked me, 'Mommy, why is there a bumble bee in my tummy?'"

"Remember B?" I ask. "B" is our name for Hudson, our eldest.

Leslie has been storing this one up all day, just waiting to tell me. "Okay," she says with a huge grin, "Hudson came up to me today and announced that he is going to adopt two children from Haiti when he turns nineteen. And then he said, 'Momma, that means you will be a grandma. So, do you want my kids to call you Grandma or Granny?'"

This simple little tradition is a little bit of heaven for us. For those of you that have children, I highly recommend trying this nightly routine of cherishing.

But this is where God has been pressing me. He has taken this little tradition and asked me to expand it beyond my own family. I remember my children, and I'm fully aware of their needs. But there are others God wants me to remember.

Here's a short list that God helped me compile this past week:

He's asking me to not just remember Avy Rosie, but to also remember Cordero, a little seven-year-old boy with Down syndrome begging on the streets of Mexico City.

He's asking me to not just remember Dubber-Dooey, but to remember Zella, a six-year-old girl in Central America standing on a slave block and being auctioned off to the highest bidder.

He's asking me to not just remember Harper Grace, but

to remember Kadokechi, an eight-year-old boy who was forced at gunpoint to kill his mother and sister and then was enslaved as a child soldier in the Lord's Resistance Army of Uganda.

He's asking me to not just remember B, but to remember Emily, a little unborn baby sucking her thumb and kicking inside the womb of her fifteen-year-old mother but is scheduled for execution at the hands of an abortion doctor tomorrow afternoon.

God wants to expand me.

He wants to expand you.

We don't have what it takes to properly remember these precious children, but God who lives within every Christian *does* have what it takes. And He is asking to take our hearts and make them feel precisely what His Father's heart is feeling.

It Begins with Ab

The first word in an alphabetical listing of all Hebrew words used in the Old Testament is *ab*. It simply means "father." What an appropriate word to begin a language!

The word *ab* is also an onomatopoeia, meaning that it sounds like what it means, for the word *ab* is the first labial sound that a newborn infant makes. It's an amazing thought that every newborn speaks a bit of Hebrew, at least enough to proclaim to the world the name of their Creator.

In the New Testament, we read of the first sounds uttered by the hearts of those adopted into the family of Jesus Christ:

*And because you are sons, God has sent forth the
Spirit of his Son into your hearts, crying out, "Abba,
Father!"* (Galatians 4:6)

How poetic, how perfect — *abba* being the intimate
form of *ab*, as *Daddy* or *Papa* are the intimate forms
of *Father*. These are the first sounds our souls make to
proclaim the realities of the new birth. And I believe that
this precious word will prove the first utterance of the
Church of Jesus Christ as we regain our rescuing swagger
and heroic gait. As the Church once again comes back to
the heart of the Father, we will be changed. Our love will
be forced to expand, our hearts compelled to increase
in size and capacity.

When the Church once again whispers, "Ab" — when
we start beholding our Ab, when we begin to study the
heart of our Ab — we will become like our Ab. We will
love like our Ab. We will give like our Ab. We will adopt
like our Ab. And we will spend our lives for the sake of
rescuing the weak, just as our Ab has done.

It says of our Ab in the Scriptures that He is a Father
to the fatherless. And when we are made new by our Ab's
abounding grace, we then become, in a real-world way,
the fulfillment of that Scripture in our day.

We become fathers to the fatherless.

Hudson's Solution

When my eldest, Hudson, was three and a half years old,
he proposed a solution to the worldwide orphan problem.
His "solution" was so childlike, so simple, so obvious,
and so deeply convicting. At the time I was producing

a three-minute weekly radio spot with Moody Radio out of Chicago. Leslie and I were so moved that I injected Hudson's childlike thought into my weekly spot, and to this day, the transcript of that three-minute segment stirs me, inspires me, and begs me to do more:

> Hudson, our little three-year old boy, heard Leslie and I talking about orphans in Haiti the other day. We were working on a plan to go down there and visit, and we were hoping to bring Hudson with us. So he started asking questions. "What's an orphan, Mommy? What made them orphans, Daddy? Can we bring them back here and have them live with us?"
>
> I have been deeply moved over these past couple days watching Hudson's childlike passion unfold for these precious children in Haiti.
>
> He is so startled by the reality that there are children in this world that don't have a mommy and a daddy, and he desperately wants to share his personal mommy and daddy with these little ones.
>
> Last night he declared, "We need to make room for these orphans, Daddy!" And he set up beds for orphans all throughout our house. Each bed consisted of a blanket, a pillow, and a stuffed animal donated from Hudson's personal collection.
>
> I walked into my bedroom last night and there on the floor was one of Hudson's baby blankets, along

with a pillow and Hudson's favorite stuffed animal doggy. He was giving up his very best for this little orphan he didn't even yet know.

As I was putting him to bed last night, I observed three different "orphan beds" neatly arranged upon the floor of his room. It was amazing to see the personal sacrifice he is willing to endure to help these orphans. To him, there is simply no question about it: if little orphans need homes, then look no further than our home. If little orphans need a mommy and daddy, then why not take the perfectly good mommy and daddy in our home and make them the mommy and daddy to a whole bunch more?

Hudson has challenged me to rethink my approach to the orphan crisis. He is willing to give up everything precious in his life to help these little ones. He will give his best stuffed animals to the cause and throw his own mommy and daddy into the kitty. Every extra square foot within his tiny room is offered up for the sake of the fatherless.

As I tucked him in last night, Hudson said, "Know what, Daddy?"

"What, Snuggle-bunny?"

His left eyebrow raised as if an amazing idea were finding wings within his mind, and he said, "If we bring these orphans into our family, then they won't be orphans anymore!"

He's right. The orphan problem is huge — 163 million fatherless kiddos are a lot to deal with. However, the solution might very well be something a three-year old could come up with. So I repeat the simple wisdom of my little boy: "If we bring these orphans into our family, then they won't be orphans anymore!"

May we all regain the simplicity of a child in order to see what must be done. Too often, it's only our children who feel the injustice and somehow intrinsically know that something is wrong when a child is left to fend for himself.

Hudson can fit three little orphans in his room.

How many orphan beds do you have room for?

While women weep as they do now, I'll fight; while little children go hungry as they do now, I'll fight; while men go to prison, in and out, in and out, as they do now, I'll fight; while there is a drunkard left, while there is a poor lost girl on the streets, while there remains one dark soul without the light of God, I'll fight—I'll fight to the very end.

William Booth

SARANDON VERSUS STUDD

Ask Susan Sarandon her motivation for helping to feed hungry kids in Africa, and she will probably say something like, "For a better world, a better tomorrow." It's the standard response of any secular superstar with a heart for humanitarian causes.

Then ask C. T. Studd why he gave up his life as a famous athlete from a wealthy family to serve the people of China, India, and later, central Africa. His answer: "I want to see the African world turned upside down for Jesus Christ!"

You see, the secular humanitarian wants a better world *without* Jesus. The Christian, on the other hand, knows that a better world comes only from people finding Jesus, being changed by Jesus, and being filled with Jesus.

The dictionary's definition of *humanitarianism* reveals a lot: "Humanitarianism is the doctrine that humankind may become perfect without divine aid." You see, the humanitarian and the Christian are both interested in fighting for the weak and vulnerable, clothing the naked, binding up the wounds of the destitute, and even adopting the abandoned and orphaned. But Sarandon and Studd are worlds apart in their motives.

Humanitarian aid can only go so far toward solving the problems caused by human injustice. Billions of dollars of foreign aid have been poured into Haiti over the last five decades, and yet Haiti's problems are much the same as, if not worse than, they were fifty years ago. Immediate needs are being met by well-meaning humanitarian groups, but no true long-term solutions have been offered. That's because Haiti (and the rest of the world) cannot get by on human aid alone. They need Jesus Christ.

The family of God has a job to do. But it can be accomplished only with the aid of the almighty Divine One. As Christians, we are not just about clothing, feeding, sheltering, and educating. We are about Jesus. If this world is well clothed, well fed, well sheltered, and well educated but still without Jesus, their eternal destiny remains darkened by the horrors of hell.

So let me be uncomfortably blunt: the world's only hope for the future lies with Jesus Christ, not in a united, well-meaning humanity.

God uses people. God uses people to perform His work. He does not send angels. Angels weep over it, but God does not use angels to accomplish His purposes. He uses burdened broken-hearted, weeping men and women.

David Wilkerson

CHAPTER FOUR

STARTING WITH ONE

You cannot get close to the Father's heart without it deeply affecting you. Not long ago, Leslie and I brushed up against it in a way that turned our world upside down. And, as the saying goes, we were forever ruined for the ordinary.

Ordinary Christianity is simply no longer an option when you encounter God's tender heart. We knew we had to *do* something. We had to respond to the Father's ache that had found its way into our own hearts.

In early 2007, Leslie spent two months studying everything she could about destitute and vulnerable children around the world. Every day she would cry as she studied, and every night she would share her findings with me. She told me stories of street children in South America, little-girl sex slaves in Cambodia, boy soldiers in Uganda, orphans in Romania, death houses in North Korea, foster kids stuck in the system in America, vulnerable children in Haiti — the list went on and on and on. We would sit there dumbfounded, struggling to know what to think, what to feel, and — most importantly — what to do.

We were angry but not sure who we were angry with. We were bewildered that we had been unaware of the extent of suffering. We would rise up and say things like, "How come no one ever told us?" And then we would settle back down in our chairs and swallow the fact that maybe someone had and we just hadn't wanted to hear it.

We were stirred. We were on the edge of our seats, ready to act. But even in the midst of our zeal and newfound passion to do something, we had never felt so small, so insignificant, so ill-equipped.

Seeing Our Smallness

A basic truth about the heroic life is that it must first know its smallness.

That isn't to say that a singular life can't make a difference. Quite the contrary. But in order for your life to become a "game changer," you must recognize that saving the world is not a man-sized task but a God-sized one.

Your job as a Christian isn't to rescue everyone, change everything, and be the father, mother, and salvation to every last child on earth. But you must realize that God is asking each of us, as individuals, to rise up and do our part.

It's okay to recognize your smallness. It's okay to feel insufficient for the task. It's okay to come face to face with the dwarfishness of your personal ability to solve this massive problem. Because it's when we see our inability that we are finally able to see God's ability.

After all, isn't He the One who measured the waters of

this earth in the hollow of His hand, meted out heaven with a span, comprehended the dust of the earth in a measure, and weighed the mountains in scales and the hills in a balance? To Him, the nations are as a drop in a bucket and are counted as the small dust of the balance (Isaiah 40:12). When He heads off to war, there are none that can stay His hand (Daniel 4:35). He sits as King between the cherubim, above all, over all, and in control of all — Creator of the heavens and the earth and Lord of all the kingdoms of this earth (Isaiah 37:16). He can bind the sweet Pleiades and loose the bands of Orion. He can set the dominion of His ordinances in the earth. He can send forth lightning, number the clouds, and stay the bottles of heaven (Job 38). He is the mighty God (Isaiah 9:6), the everlasting God (Isaiah 40:28). He is God blessed forever (Romans 9:5), the God of the whole earth (Isaiah 54:5), and His throne is for ever and ever (Hebrews 1:8). He is the Almighty who is, who was, and who is to come (Revelation 1:8).

Any questions?

We may be unable to alter this world, but He can.

He is able to rescue. He is able to change everything.

He is able to take one paltry obedient life like yours and make a footprint that is a million times larger than your actual shoe size.

The hero's life is simply a life that knows its smallness and yet strides forward with a clear picture of God's bigness.

Starting with One

Leslie and I realized we couldn't take on the corrupt death squads in Brazil, the Lord's Resistance Army in

Uganda, the sex-trafficking industry in southeast Asia, and fix the foster care system in America all at the same time.

There are 163 million orphaned children, and there are only two of us. Our home simply isn't big enough.

There are 27 million human slaves, and there aren't enough hours in a day, days in a week, weeks in a year, and years left in our lives to rescue every single one of them.

An estimated 150,000 people are dying daily without knowing Jesus Christ, and Leslie and I can't possibly help every one of them.

Every day in China, 35,000 female babies are aborted. And every day in America, 23,000 more are added to the death tally. We simply cannot save them all.

Since we can't do everything, should we do *nothing?*

Getting close to the Father's heart at first seems overwhelming, but God is so gentle in the way He builds His saints. He doesn't assign them tasks they can't fulfill. He doesn't set them up for failure but, rather, He sets them up to triumph and to make a palpable difference in this world.

He does this by starting us out with *one.*

One simple prayer to begin praying.

One singular life to help.

When God looks at the trouble of this world, He doesn't see a mass of 163 million orphans. He sees 163 million individuals who are suffering. He knows each of their names. He knows every cry of their delicate hearts and every thought inside their minds. He feels their every pang of hunger, and He identifies with their rejection, their loneliness, their heartaches, their pain, and their diseases.

So when He calls His saints to move forward, He

introduces us not to a cause but to *real* children with *real* names, *real* feelings, and *real* pain. Yes, it's a cause, but it's not the nobility of a cause that moves our Father in heaven; it's the plight of individual souls that stirs His heart.

Our God thinks of each of us as *one*. One worth dying for. One worth giving everything to rescue. One who is loved so much that the precious blood of Jesus Christ was shed in order to redeem us, to purchase us for His own. Our God is a personal God: He sees each one, He feels for each one, and He does whatever it takes to reach each one. And it's a startling realization for each of us to discover that we *are* that one.

He rescues us, washes us clean, and sets our feet on a solid rock. He fortifies us and makes us strong so that He can then pour us out to reach another one just like us.

That's heroism.

A hero is someone (someone just like you) who has been rescued, washed, reformed, and built up by the grace of Almighty God and turned outward to see the plight of this dying world, and then sent forth as a rescuer to stand in the gap and take the hit for the little ones.

That is what Jesus did. And that's what the men and women who follow Jesus are called to do.

Our Little Harper

Leslie and I spent three months praying daily for direction. With so many battlefronts at hand, how do you choose? With so many children, so many needs to be met, how do you know where and how to respond?

By April 2007, we decided on our first step. It wasn't much, but it was something we could *do*. We decided to visit the nearest international adoption agency and ask how we could help. We didn't have the money available to adopt a child, so that seemed to be out of the question. But we did have a platform and a measure of influence we could possibly use. We had time, energy, hands, and feet, and maybe there was a way that we could put these to some practical use.

The night before we visited the adoption agency, Leslie and I talked about our upcoming adventure. "I'm not sure we should look at any of their pictures," I said, "because I've heard so many stories about people seeing a picture and being emotionally stirred."

"You don't want to look at any pictures?" Leslie asked.

"This is research," I said. "We simply don't have any money to put toward adoption."

"How long would it take for us to save up?"

"If we lived on beans and rice and scraped together every spare coin, I figure two years."

So we decided to make this visit a "research only" trip. And that meant no pictures.

The following day we drove thirty minutes to the adoption agency. We were a bit nervous. There was a sense of expectancy in the air, but we had no clue what awaited us. This particular agency specialized in Korean and Chinese adoptions. The adoption counselor sat down with us in a side office to discuss our options. Since we weren't interested in typical adoption services, we proved somewhat of a difficult case. We really just wanted information. We were waiting to hear something that would cause us to say, "That's it!" We figured it would be some sort of service activity, some sort of visitation concept, or maybe some kind of practical help we could provide to the agency itself.

We were told it would take approximately two and a half years to adopt a child from either Korea or China. And there was a waiting list of nearly 100 families. Leslie and I looked at each other briefly and then shook our heads in the negative. That wasn't it. Not only did we not have the financial resources, but there were already a hundred couples waiting to help. We knew we were looking for a clear area of need.

We talked for another fifteen or so minutes about the adoption process until I started to shift in my seat. I gathered my keys, wallet, and phone that were sitting on the table and subconsciously prepared to bring the discussion to a close. Adoption sounded great, but not for a couple of years. And even then, it would need to be something clearly marked by God. This just didn't seem to have the seal of the Almighty upon it.

That was when Leslie asked the question that changed the course of our lives: "Are there any other children?"

"Well," the counselor said, "we do have waiting children."

"What are 'waiting children'?"

"Waiting children are children that have been approved for adoption by their country's governments," answered the counselor, "but have been passed over by our list of waiting parents due to the fact that they are either older or because they have special needs."

"What do you mean by special needs?" Leslie asked.

"Oh, special needs can be any number of things," said the counselor. "Physical deformities, mental retardation, Down syndrome, cleft pallet, blindness, deafness, etc."

Then she had a thought. "For instance, we have a two-month-old girl on our waiting list right now who was born without fingers, a club foot, and deformities on her right foot."

"So," I interjected, finding a pressing interest in this line of discussion, "are you saying that these children are available for adoption but no one is wanting to adopt them?"

"That's correct."

"What happens to them if no one adopts them?"

"Each child is given a window of time in which a family here in the States can adopt them," she clarified, "and if that window passes and no one steps forward in adoptive response, then that child is institutionalized for life."

Leslie and I sat there, silent, attempting to process this information. There is something about the word *institutionalized* that is difficult to swallow.

The counselor must have noticed that a chord had been struck, because she said, "As for the two-month old girl without fingers — do you want to see her picture?"

I was quick to nix that notion. After all, we had agreed to a strict no-pictures policy. This was an information-only inquiry.

"How about if I just show you a picture of her hands?" she offered.

Well, that sounded perfectly harmless to me. Hands were hands. It was the faces of the little ones that tie you up emotionally. A picture of a pair of hands sounded very much in keeping with information gathering.

"Sure," I said, after a brief consulting glance at Leslie.

A couple of minutes later, I was looking at an 8x10 photograph of little Harper's eight-day-old hands, and suddenly this became personal. This became emotional. This became *real* to me. The father heart of God was roused within me, and this little girl became important to me. I was staring at two tiny hands, and in those hands were a story. A story of this little girl's abandonment. A story of being passed over by a hundred families. A story of someone the world saw as imperfect but whom God saw as perfectly precious.

The photo was grainy and lacking in professional quality. But to this day it's one of the most powerful, most beautiful pictures I have ever beheld.

As I stared at the photo, I was silent. I knew I had to get out of there. I didn't want to cry in front of this counselor. I told Leslie that I thought we should go and "consider these things," and we respectfully dismissed ourselves from the meeting.

We gathered our things and headed out to our car. I didn't say a word as I walked. I knew that if I spoke I would start sobbing. This was a manly dignity thing — I didn't want to do my weeping anywhere but in private.

This was it. I could feel it.

I was sensing the Father's heart thumping in my chest. This little girl was His girl. This little girl needed a father. And even though I had only seen her hands, I cared about this little girl as only a father can. God was expanding my heart. As I drove home, away from the photo and the adoption agency, my heart increased in capacity.

My pocketbook didn't stretch. Money didn't just suddenly appear in my bank account, but love grew in my heart. And where there is a father's love, anything is possible. There is no barrier that can't be breached, no mountain that can't be scaled, and no canyon that can't be bridged.

I cried the entire trip home, with one sentence playing upon my lips: "A father to the fatherless … God sets the solitary in families" (Psalm 68:5–6).

The cost was $27,535 for Leslie and me to help this little girl. That would be five years of living on beans and rice and squirreling away every spare coin. And yet, if we were going to help her, we needed to come up with $15,535 in three weeks' time. We would then need the remaining $12,000 within a few months.

What does a father do? Panic? Give up? Throw in the towel? Reason it all away? No. A father must trust that God backs those who reach out to His little ones.

In the words of Oswald Chambers, "When we deliberately choose to obey God, He will tax the remotest star and the last grain of sand to assist us with all His Almighty Power."

I can tell you, *this* father prayed. I prayed like I had never prayed before. My prayer went something like this: "God, You are the one asking us to do this. Therefore, I am asking You to supply the needed funds. I ask this unashamedly, boldly, and straightforwardly. And I will not stop asking until every dime comes in."

Hours every day were spent praying for this seemingly impossible provision. We told only a handful of people about our situation. Two of those people were Leslie's parents. Her parents were so moved by the notion of their granddaughter currently living on the other side of the world and in need that they wrote a letter to all their friends. It simply said, "Our granddaughter is on the other side of the world. If you would like to help bring her home, please send your support [here]."

Leslie and I honestly didn't expect much to come of that letter, but it generated such a wave of support that on the day we needed to write the check, we had miraculously received a total of $15,500.

And after writing the big check to the adoption agency, we returned home and Leslie prepared to write a $35 check to our babysitter. The sitter waved her hand when Leslie held out the check to her and said, "No, put it towards your adoption fund."

On the day we needed it, only three weeks from the day we had walked into the agency and saw that photograph, we had received the precise amount we needed to the penny. And in the months to come, the other $12,000 somehow found its way to us.

We didn't put one dime toward Harper's adoption.

We simply said yes, and God did the rest.

God started us out with *one*. He said, *Don't focus on the 163 million. Focus on the one. Love this one. Serve this one. Adopt this one.*

God's calling for each of us is both small and great. It is small in the sense that it is made up of tiny steps of obedience — little decisions that in and of themselves aren't very big or grand. And the calling is great in the sense that in these little steps is found the power to turn the world on its head.

God has a "Harper-sized" step for you. It's just big enough to completely alter your life and prove the extraordinary faithfulness of God, yet just small enough that you can, in good conscience, say yes and know that you are truly going to prove helpful through your obedience.

Many of us have stopped believing in a God who works miracles. But that's because we are not allowing God to put us in situations that would prove Him to be a miracle-working God. If you want to see the supernatural power, faithfulness, and provision of God, reach out and help someone who is vulnerable and in need. Feed the hungry. Clothe the naked. Adopt the orphan. Make the widow's heart sing for joy. Visit the imprisoned. Share the Gospel with the lost. Comfort the mourners. And labor to set the enslaved free.

When you set out to do Hero Work, you will find that the Great Hero Himself will come and make your obedience His intimate business.

You must do it! You cannot hold back.
You have enjoyed yourself in Christianity long enough.
You have had pleasant feelings, pleasant songs, pleasant
meetings, pleasant prospects. There has been much of
human happiness, much clapping of hands and shouting
of praises — very much of heaven on earth. Now then,
go to God and tell Him you are prepared as much as
necessary to turn your back upon it all, and that you are
willing to spend the rest of your days
struggling in the midst of these perishing
multitudes, whatever it may cost you.

William Booth

But when you do a charitable deed, do not let your left
hand know what your right hand is doing, that your
charitable deed may be in secret; and your Father who
sees in secret will Himself reward you openly.

Matthew 6:3-4

KISSING BABIES FOR THE CAMERAS

When natural disaster strikes in this world, the Reverend Jesse Jackson gets on a plane and flies straight to the epicenter. He gathers the camera crews and says, "Roll 'em boys!" He then proceeds to kiss all the babies in the vicinity, shake hands with the powers that be, and then gives a short, moving speech about how tragic the situation is.

On the one hand, I appreciate the reverend's desire to draw attention to the plight of people in need. It's very thoughtful of him. But most of us recognize politicking when we see it. Politicking seeks to do the right thing — in front of the cameras, of course — but the motive behind the doing of that right thing can often be called into question.

If you are thinking about responding to the message of

this book, please do. But don't respond like a politician. Leave the television crews behind. Go ahead — kiss the babies and shake the hands of the powers that be. Even give a speech, for all I care. But please don't do it to win a vote back home.

If you are envisioning photo ops, plaudits, lights and cameras, and front-page headlines for your charitable work, then you need to take time to consider your motives prior to launching out.

True Hero's work is done for an audience of One. A true Hero is willing to serve the withered, aging drug addict in the back alleys of Bombay without receiving recognition. A true Hero is willing to go to the most obscure corners of this earth and wash feet day in and day out without being accompanied by a biographer, a journalist, or a filmmaker.

If your work is really all about doing what Jesus would do, then prove it.

This world is sick and tired of politicians. There is a desperate need for humble saints who don't care a whit if their work is ever noticed by the people around them. They do what they do for the smile of their Father in heaven alone, and not to win the votes of a human constituency.

If you read history, you will find that the Christians who did most for the present world were just those who thought most of the next. The Apostles themselves who set on foot the conversion of the Roman Empire, the great men who built up the Middle Ages, the English Evangelicals who abolished the Slave Trade, all left their mark on Earth precisely because their minds were occupied with Heaven. It is since Christians have largely ceased to think of the other world that they have become so ineffective in this.

C.S. Lewis
Mere Christianity

CHAPTER FIVE

SPIRITUAL EMPLOYMENT

Finding Work in the Father's Business

I work with myriad twenty-somethings as the president of a Bible college, and as a result I am surrounded by the vigor of youthful zeal. And, I must tell you, I am amazed at what God is doing in this younger generation. Whereas, many of us threw up our hands a decade ago and accepted that this next generation is morally without hope, I am witnessing something beautiful amid this vortex of postmodern Godlessness.

Nearly sixty percent of our graduates at Ellerslie Discipleship Training are seriously planning on adopting at least one child in addition to having their own biological children. In addition, more than ninety percent of our graduates are either planning on adopting or would be very open to adopting sometime in the future. I don't know about you, but that's a huge a shift in thinking from my collegiate days.

The number of Ellerslie students who want to do orphan-related ministry is startling. The number of our students choosing to labor on behalf of the enslaved, trafficked, and abused is deeply encouraging. The number of students willing to do whatever is necessary on behalf of the unborn makes you seriously wonder if a significant revival is on the horizon.

With all this fervor for service and self-sacrifice to address the priorities of the Father's heart, our greatest challenge isn't finding a way to motivate our students; it is helping to direct and harness the zeal and enthusiasm of our students. Our students aren't just *ready* to do something; they MUST do something. They are chomping at the bit to *go*, to *do*, to *help*, and to somehow be a picture of Jesus to this dying world.

Our challenge is supplying opportunity to those interested in serving. Our students are saying, "I don't care about getting paid; I just want to serve."

I have an army in Windsor, Colorado, ready to do something. But the challenge we face in modern Christianity at large, and the problem we are facing at Ellerslie, is a need for tactical coordination to help the saints serve effectively.

At Ellerslie, we call this itch to do something the need for "spiritual employment." We have a massive spiritual unemployment rate in and among the rank and file of the Christian community. There are millions of Christians willing and ready to serve with no clear avenue through which to do so. American Christians, in particular, need to work off that blubbery belly of spiritual lethargy, but they don't know where to start.

I'm convinced that the formation of spiritual employment represents one of the single greatest needs in the North American Church. We must have opportunity, training, and encouragement to get Christians to turn outside themselves. We have a crisis of spiritual unemployment, and that leads to a definite frustration amongst ready saints.

"I want to do something," students tell me, "but I don't know what to do." I understand their frustration. I have struggled with it and wrestled with it in my own life. But I'm convinced that God never wastes a willing saint.

The answer for your own spiritual unemployment may not be immediately evident. But if you will take your unemployment issues to the feet of the King and simply lay them there—if you make your voice heard in the heavenly courts saying, "God, please bend me, prepare me, and make me useful to You"—you can be certain of one thing: He will.

Are You a Ministry Starter?

Spiritual unemployment is an issue that goes beyond us as individuals. In many ways, it's a corporate dilemma. So in your praying, don't just ask God to supply you with a clear-cut job description—ask Him to open up the business for *all* the ready saints on this earth today.

There are those in the Body of Christ who can help answer this prayer. They are built by God to supply "employment" for others. They are ministry starters, and they can help provide innovative opportunities through which others can serve.

There are others in the Body who are built to be responders. The responders work best when someone creates a doorway for them to walk through and begin to serve. At Ellerslie, we are laboring to create opportunities for our graduates, and it is truly exciting to see what is happening as a result. But we can't meet the demands of the entire Church. There is a significant need today for ministry starters.

One of my favorite ministries laboring on the front lines to create spiritual employment opportunities is called His Little Feet. At Ellerslie, we work closely with His Little Feet by providing housing to orphan children while they are in the States. The founders of His Little Feet, Mike and Christa Hahn, are passionate about supplying spiritual employment to those who encounter their ministry.

"We don't just want to tell American Christians about the plight of orphans," says Christa. "We want to give them practical opportunities to really reach out to the orphans."

Mike adds, "It's only when we touch the orphan issue personally that we become agents of change for these vulnerable children. If people can actually visit these countries and see the needs up close, it makes the need real instead of just theoretical."

Imagine not just knowing about the orphan crisis but personally touching it, seeing it, and interacting with it. In order to connect Christians like you and me with real children with real names and real stories, His Little Feet supplies opportunities to sponsor children and build real-life relationships with them. And, of course, they are helping people adopt little ones from all over the world.

This is the kind of thinking the Church needs today.

If you are able, be a ministry starter — a spiritual recruitment agency, if you will — for the Father's business. True, not all of us are built to be ministry starters, but every one of us can be an encourager, a gift-giver, and a practical servant to those who are reaching out to change the lives of these vulnerable children. One of the great exhortations within the adoption community is if you are not personally in a position to adopt, then you should be helping someone who is.

However, because adoption is just one way of being about the Father's business in this world, I think this exhortation should be expanded to read like this: if you are not personally in a position to preach the Gospel, set the captive free, deliver the poor, clothe the naked, put the "solitary" in a family, make the widow's heart sing for joy, heal the sick, comfort the weak, or rescue the victim from the teeth of evildoers — then you should be helping someone who is.

In Conclusion

Be recklessly willing to move outside of yourself. Yes, it will mean a change in your life, a change in your priorities. But you will never regret it. Let Jesus take the helm and do in and through your life the same thing He did while He was here on earth — the Father's business.

Don't start by trying to save 163 million. Start with *one*. Don't let yourself become overwhelmed by the numbers, the obstacles, and the seemingly undefeatable powers of darkness. Start with one and let God prove His power, His faithfulness, and His love to you through that first baby-step of obedience.

And don't be discouraged if it takes a bit of time for your work to fully come together. But don't accept spiritual unemployment. That's not an option. So keep your prayer life sharp and keep your eyes open to see what God is seeing and feel what He is feeling.

The world's problems will not be solved in a day. Yet amazingly, the answer for all our dilemmas is available to everyone and every situation on this great big globe in the person of Jesus Christ. He is the answer to every problem — bar none.

The world needs Jesus.

If you are willing to be His hands and feet to this lost and dying world, then please feel welcomed into the sacred fellowship of burning hearts. Know that those of us standing for the glory of Jesus Christ do not stand alone. Though we may feel alone, though we may work alone, though we may wonder if our individual contributions are making a bit of difference in this world, we are never alone. The Lord is with us, and He is recruiting an army of men and women with a fiery desire to see the Lamb that was slain receive the full reward for His suffering.

Deo juvante! With God's help!

Prayer is of transcendent importance. Prayer is the mightiest agent to advance God's work. Praying hearts and hands only can do God's work. Prayer succeeds when all else fails. ... To say prayers in a decent, delicate way is not heavy work. But to pray really, to pray till hell feels the ponderous stroke, to pray till the iron gates of difficulty are opened, till the mountains of obstacles are removed, till the mists are exhaled and the clouds are lifted, and the sunshine of a cloudless day brightens—this is hard work, but it is God's work, and man's best labor.

E.M. Bounds

We Christians are debtors to all men at all times in all places. Men are blind—we must lead them.
Men are bound—we must free them.
Sinful men are spiritually diseased—we must heal them.
Godless men are dead—we must raise them from the dead by the Holy Spirit's power.

Leonard Ravenhill

You must do it. With the light that is now broken in upon your mind, and the call that is now sounding in your ears, and the beckoning hands that are now before your eyes, you have no alternative. To go down among the perishing crowds is your duty. Your happiness from now on will consist in sharing their misery, your ease in sharing their pain, your crown in helping them to bear their cross, and your heaven in going into the very jaws of hell to rescue them.

William Booth

ABOUT THE AUTHOR

There were three things growing up that Eric Ludy declared he would never become: a teacher, a missionary, and a pastor. He became all three. In a vain attempt to gain some credibility he also became a writer. But seventeen books later, he's admitted that this plan backfired big time — the messages contained in his books have led to more scorn than the other three combined. Ludy is the president of Ellerslie Mission Society, the teaching pastor at the Church at Ellerslie, and the lead instructor in the Ellerslie Discipleship Training. He is descended from seven generations of pastors, totally uncool, somewhat skinny, and in Japan supposedly his last name means "Nerd." But, that said, he is clothed in the shed blood of His beloved Savior; Leslie, his wife of twenty years, still laughs at his jokes; and his six kids think he is Superman (or at least Clark Kent). So, all is well with the author of this book. He calls Windsor, Colorado home, but longs for his real home in Heaven where being a "fool for Christ" finally will be realized to be the most brilliant life-decision any human has ever made.

EricLudy.com

MORE BOOKS FROM ERIC LUDY

Romance, Relationships, & Purity
When God Writes Your Love Story
When Dreams Come True
Meet Mr. Smith
A Perfect Wedding
The First 90 Days of Marriage
Teaching True Love to a Sex-at-13 Generation
It Takes a Gentleman and a Lady

Godly Manhood
God's Gift to Women
Christian Living & Discipleship
When God Writes Your Life Story
The Bravehearted Gospel
Heroism

Prayer
Wrestling Prayer

Memoirs & Confessions
Are These Really My Pants?
Evolution of the Pterodactyl
The Bold Return of the Dunces
Fingerprints of Grace

EricLudy.com

DISCOVER MORE
FROM THE AUTHOR

SERMONS

Unashamed Gospel Thunder.

Listen now: Ellerslie.com/sermons

CONFERENCES

Come expectant. Leave transformed.

Learn more: Ellerslie.com/conferences

DISCIPLESHIP TRAINING

A set apart season to become firmly
planted in Christ.

Learn more: Ellerslie.com/training

READ MORE FROM ERIC LUDY

EricLudy.com

Made in the USA
San Bernardino, CA
11 November 2015